Green
Panties,
Ulcers
& Corns

Green Panties, Ulcers & Corns

COMMITMENT, SACRIFICE AND RESPONSIBILITY OF WOMEN IN SERVANT LEADERSHIP

Necole K. Muhammad, LCSW

purposely created PUBLISHING

This book is dedicated to God, my mother, my father, my husband, my two adult children, my extended family, my sorors, my mentors, my friends, my former students, and my clients. Everything I am is because of you. My tribe challenges me to grow and develop in ways that continuously reintroduce me to myself. This journey keeps me excited and always coming back for more.

Table of Contents

Introduction

Green Panties, Ulcers, & Corns

9 Lessons in Sacrifice, Self-Preservation, and Servant Leadership

My mother, Mrs. Leaster Joyce Robinson-Fonville, was the first woman I saw as a servant leader in my community. I watched and unknowingly took notes every day on how she carried herself and on how it looked and what it meant to be a strong and well-rounded woman in a variety of circumstances. I wanted to be just like her, but with my own special seasoning. I had no clue while under her roof that her mentoring, coaching, discipline, and counseling would last well into my adulthood molding me into who I am today. I am beyond grateful that she is the vessel through whom God chose for me to come. I can vividly remember the day my life made a significant shift. I had to be about 11 years old. It was a few days before Thanksgiving when my mother came home very enthusiastic from work and said that we would be going to the neighborhood hospital to help prepare baskets for the needy. She pulled me in close and explained that we must be conscious of how blessed we were and the importance of helping others who were not as fortunate.

I knew that there were people in need, but nowhere in my mind did I have a point a reference for community service and what this actually meant. I secretly but immediately became irritated, because I would much rather have been with my friends. After all, that was more important. We left home and arrived at the hospital where we were directed to a large conference room. Food and other items were scattered at different stations to be placed into each basket for the individuals in need. I did not know the people in the room, and there was no one there my age, but they were all happy to see my mother. We began strategically assembling items and carefully placing them in the baskets. Once we were done, everyone who assisted was given a list of five families or more to deliver the baskets to before Thanksgiving Day. The list contained their names, how many people were in their household, their ages, their addresses, and their phone numbers. My mother received her list, and we began our journey to deliver the baskets. Every family was excited and thankful, and there was always a door full of small children. A few became emotional. I never wanted it to end.

That day changed my life forever. Without saying it out loud or even knowing what to say, I knew that I always wanted to feel what I felt that day and that I would be serving people forever. My dedication and determination to be of service created a vibration that would always manifest opportunities to serve. I intentionally signed up for events in and out of school to engage in community service, which interestingly always had a leadership component. I had no idea that those experiences prepared me for leadership positions I didn't seek.

My journey as a servant leader went up a few notches after I transitioned from being a juvenile probation officer to a school social worker. At that time, my intentional mission as a school social worker—a profession I loved—was to engage youth in every way possible to help them understand the greatness they have inside of them. That level of engagement led me to be considered for an administrative position that really exposed what I knew and what I needed to know as a servant leader. I was offered an Assistant Principal position at a Chicago Public High School that at the time was considered low performing and to some dangerous. My first year was overwhelming with meetings every day, late nights, countless events, hundreds of students to monitor, and unlimited emails and tasks. I had a lot to prove as a new administrator, and everyone was watching. After a summer full of planning, my confidence increased, and the second year was up and running. Then the unthinkable happened. A fight erupted, causing 29 students to be arrested, and somehow, it made international news. What seemed to initially be getting stronger all of a sudden became a spectacle for criticism. Praise from central office became sarcastic threats, everything was scrutinized, and meetings were cold and no longer collaborative.

This unfortunate and misunderstood event introduced me to a different side of leadership. I learned quickly that when in leadership, the buck stops with you. Leaders must have the answers because your title and salary say so, and solutions are mandatory or else. The entire team buckled up and handled it. We fought like hell against misunderstandings, disparities, blatant lies, and pushed for new opportunities, our reputation and new norms. This level of intensity went on for months that led to years in high school administration, moving from an assistant principal to a principal. The personal sacrifices and experiences led to the book you are reading now—*Green Panties, Ulcers, & Corns: 9 Lessons in Sacrifice, Self-Preservation, and Servant Leadership.* My intention is to give you insight into my experiences so that you may adopt some tools to engage in your assignment as a servant leader while being mindful of your need for self-preservation.

Lesson 1

Get Naked (What Did COVID-19 Come to Teach Me?)

In the middle of March 2020, while writing this book, I began to experience COVID-19-type symptoms that were not acknowledged at the time, nor was I able to get tested. The CDC had not listed them as possible symptoms, therefore I was left with the medical suggestion of "Just stay home. You are not severe enough for testing, and it may not be COVID-19." As I put the final touches on this book to submit for editing, I tested positive. I am currently on day 94 with lingering symptoms and another testing day on the horizon. This COVID-19 journey put several things into perspective, and I feel blessed to have been forced into a hard stop. I thought I knew based upon my experiences what self-preservation was, but I had never really stopped. I just slowed down. My revision of this book is like a rebirth of my message.

So let's go back. My wake-up call began on a beautiful spring day in 2014. I was in a phenomenal mood.

I got out of the shower and entered my bedroom to put on my favorite pair of green panties. These panties have been with me since my freshman year of college, and they made the cut at least once every two weeks. The color and style of these panties provided a special yet comforting feeling. One time, to my surprise, I put them on, and they did not just flip down. They rolled down like a pair of Carol Burnett knee highs. I was devastated that my favorite panties were screaming for relief. I sat on the side of my bed and looked in the mirror with serious disappointment. The root of this issue was obvious. I was overweight, and I had not noticed. The crazy part is that I was more upset about not being able to wear my panties than I was about the weight gain. The high level of stress, lack of self-care, unhealthy foods, and not exercising were a recipe for the inability to fit into my favorite green panties. But it did not end there.

Shortly after the panties crisis, I began to experience a gnawing pain on my right side, which led to a doctor visit and a diagnosis of an ulcer. The doctor gave suggestions about lifestyle changes and a prescription and sent me on my way. This ulcer was the second indicator of the stress, unbalanced chemicals and hormones, and the unhealthy eating to which I was exposing myself daily. While processing the weight gain with a noticeable pain on my side, I continued to handle my business without missing a beat. I still had to run the halls, walk the floors, and climb the stairs to monitor the building as a Chicago public high school administrator.

The final straw came as I began to feel an irritating pain on the top of my toes. Up until recently, I felt that my feet were the most beautiful feet that the creator put on the planet earth. One evening, I removed my so-called well thought out footwear and began to unveil what would ultimately push me over the cliff. I had developed two corns on each foot. What the hell? Somebody, please take the wheel! These notable issues were indicators at the tip of the iceberg of self-neglect and psychosocial issues that ravaged through my being. It highlighted a part of the cost of "by any means necessary" leadership that I pray you never experience.

Prior to writing this book, I was one of twenty-one talented authors who wrote the best-selling book, *Soul Talk, Volume 3*. The success of that book gave me the confidence to write a book that had been stirring in me for the past five years. Pre-COVID-19, I thought I was so clear about what I wanted to convey to you, and then our whole world came to a hard stop. The silence was so loud that after I unconditionally accepted the experience, I could finally hear myself think. I'm not sure what I thought I knew before, but this life-changing situation took away 95 percent of my distractions. I got an opportunity to audit what was really important and how I really, really felt about the lessons learned in leadership. When my symptoms grew stronger and I couldn't focus, I submitted to the process to heal, rest, and reflect. This was really the best chance for me to "get naked," remove all facades, go deep, and stop faking the funk.

I asked myself, "What did COVID-19 come to teach me?" I hadn't ever gone this deep; I am now in unchartered but very calm territory. I was working from home with no sorority or other organizational meetings to attend and no one knocking on my door. It became clear to me that even though I resigned as a high school principal in 2018, I had unknowing moved from one rat race to the next over a nine-year period. What was driving me? What I have found in my journey is that transparency sometimes causes with trouble. Was I ready to see my—*self*? Was I ready to take responsibility for my style of leadership? I love being a servant leader, but I also want to make sure I show up as a leader and not as a representative. This level of reflection helps you to grow and give yourself permission to release some parts of yourself that represent a protector but may really be slowly ruining you, even with the best intentions.

Looking back, I can clearly hear the quote "be careful what you wish for." For months in 2011, I sat in a small windowless room every day, praying, meditating, and asking God to use me to help people live on their highest level. He did just that, which reminds me of motivational speaker and author, Lisa Nichols' statement that "some of your best gifts come wrapped in sandpaper." Just as I thought I was going to make my next move as a school social worker in another district, the principal at my assigned school asked me to think about being an assistant principal. In the back of my mind, I'm thinking, "Who, me? I've never been a teacher. They won't respect me. I'm not prepared for this type of responsibility. The principal informed me that the school was the recipient of a three-year grant and that the assistant principal position that I would fill was for student development and intervention. After having this conversation, I prayed and had a conversation with my husband. This opportunity was not something I asked for. Or had I? I asked to serve and empower people to live on their highest level and be in alignment with God's assignment. I didn't specifically ask to be a high school administrator, but the way it was delivered, I needed to be laser-focused on the mission and not the position.

I was so green, but I created a façade of confidence. When I look back, I relied on my observations, a great team, and quick thinking to handle the majority of issues that popped up on a daily basis. I was forced to learn quickly about the academic side from the principal, the assistant principal of curriculum and instruction, teachers, and students. I played a major role in molding and shaping youth who will be our future leaders. This was not taken lightly; my goal was to be the best in my assignment while growing and developing as a servant leader. I dove in head first and went full speed to lead and be a student at the same time. As time passed, so many lessons were learned, and despite my hard work with my head held high, I was walking around like a well-dressed onion, and I really wasn't taking care of myself and my personal business. The task was so big that there was no room for things beyond my mission.

I was a married mother of two high school students, a daughter, an assistant principal, a principal, doctoral student, and then me. The sad part is that all of these beautiful blessings were sacrificed because the idea of being a leader was more than a notion. These blessings were always hovering like a dark cloud in the back of my head, and the burden was emotionally heavy. Here I was asking people to be socially and emotionally together and to live their lives on their highest level yet, my life was being sustained on a toothpick foundation.

Responsibility and leadership in your own life are necessary to authentically help those around you. These two worlds stretched me to the brink, and I needed to make a decision or the things I claimed I valued the most would inevitably be lost. I embraced the theory that I needed to have some help. Who helps the helper? I needed to have somebody in my life who was not going to allow me to live in the murky waters. I no longer wanted to pretend like everything was okay. I was not living the life that I wanted to live. I needed to get to the nitty gritty and ask myself some serious questions: Am I happy? If not, why? What can I correct? Is this really God's assignment?

But guess what? No matter how many times I asked questions, I never really looked for God to provide the answers. I kept racking my brain trying to find solutions, and despite minor successes, where it mattered the most, I failed.

Questions

1. How often do you pause to reflect on your journey?

2. Will you regret your successful journey if you lose everything on the way?

3. When was the last time you connected with *yourself*?

Lesson 2

Seamless Transitions

As far back as I can remember, it seems as though there has never been an opportunity that did not come seamlessly to me. The dots always stay connected, and the lessons and experiences seem relevant to the past, present and future. But for some reason, I seem to always forget in the midst of each and every time having to always go back and ponder about how I got there in the first place. *Green Panties, Ulcers, & Corns* is about experiences from a servant leader's position and how self-preservation is necessary in order to experience long-term success. Going back to 2010 as a school social worker, I received a phone call from a supervisor stating that I needed to make an immediate transition to a different school. This was simultaneously happening at a time when schools in the City of Chicago were falling victim to the turnaround system and everyone was on edge.

I completed my goodbyes to my clients and immediately was assigned to a high school that at the time was in complete disarray. I had to adjust to new administration that was striving to bring the school to a place of calm. This was in the middle of the school year. How was I going to fit with students who had already been through many transitions? I worked side by side with the Illinois State Board of Education transition team and a fairly new school team. The Illinois State Board of Education team was tough, expectations were high, and other people's past errors needed to be corrected immediately. There was a rapid fire of meetings, questions, assessments, and interventions that would help students improve their social-emotional balance, behavior, grades, and attendance. I was a part of a multi-disciplinary team that needed to make sure that those students who were in the highest level of need experienced academic, social, and emotional success. Our team worked well together and saw major gains in every domain.

In a short period of time, I started to become deeply engaged with the staff and the students, trying to understand every dynamic. I began putting in more hours than expected and jumped all in without asking any questions. The students' achievement was just as important to me as my own two children's. I understood that people did not see their potential. I understood the dynamics because I was from the neighborhood. Their luggage was familiar. They just could not check it at the door, so it oozed out in the halls, classrooms, and events. We had a lot of work to do, and it was my personal mission to make sure that their rights were never violated and that access and opportunities were available.

By the year 2011, I was making a decision with my family based upon a financial situation in my home to move to a different school district. I began the process and was seeking a letter of recommendation. I had become quite close with the principal and had a conversation with her requesting a letter of recommendation. She began to share with me the opportunity for the school to receive a grant. She didn't want me to leave and wished I had the credentials needed for an administration position. To her surprise, I had the credentials to become an assistant principal, but I had no plans to use it, as I did not see myself as an individual who wanted to be in charge of adults. She advised that I pray about it and talk it over with my husband. The mere fact that I had credentials on a shelf with no intention to use them sparked a conversation that led to an opportunity that I did not seek. It was worth pausing for guidance. I was ready. I accepted the offer and went through the process seamlessly with no issues or barriers. This was a sign from God that there was a mission He wanted handled. Even though I had no idea what I was getting myself into, I leaned on the alignment with this particular administration, my knowledge of and rapport with the students, and the mission from

God—not the position. Over the summer, I prepared as if I was preparing for my report card pick up with the Creator to make sure that the students would return to a competent leader and that I would not let them down. Looking back, I am very clear that when you are chosen for an assignment, the transition and experiences may not look connected, but everything about your journey will be clear that "favor ain't fair" and seamless transitions are ordained.

Questions

1. Have you found the fluency of your journey in your life transitions?

2. Have your views changed or expanded about your ordained experiences?

3. What common threads have always been present when you seamlessly transition?

Lesson 3

* ❋ ❋ *

Who Did You Have to Become?

Fights in the school had happened before, but this particular one introduced me to a part of myself that I had never met. On October 22, 2013 a large fight broke out in the school that caused us to be on the local, national, and international news. In our central leadership's eyes, we went from an administration that was making gains to a broken system that lacked control in every area. In one conversation with a consultant, I was told without hesitation that I had not made my mental transition from a school social worker to an assistant principal. She was clear that if I didn't pull it together quickly, I would fail the students and staff at this school. I didn't have a point of reference for what that meant, because all I had ever been was a school social worker. Now, I needed to become someone who could rightfully fulfill my title. I became very angry and judgmental, because at my core, I considered myself to be one of the ones who loved helping people get to the next level, and maybe she had become hardened through the years and lost her way.

What I quickly came to understand once I quieted my ego was the consultant's intention. She was a seasoned leader in the school system, and she was ultimately a vessel God used to pull my coat-tail. I put my big girl panties on and realized what was at stake. I was right beneath the principal, who had to take responsibility for everything that happened in the school. If it was not good on my level, it definitely reflected my boss's leadership, and I didn't want to be responsible for that reputation. I also needed to acknowledge the saying, "You don't know what you don't know." I had to ask some questions and do some detailed internal work to figure out who I had to become to step up to this particular assignment. I studied, researched, read books, observed individuals, and adopted practices that would be beneficial to my professional growth and position.

My movement and thoughts were intentional and laser focused. We were responsible for 1,000 plus students, approximately 150 staff, and the stakeholders who were vested in our mission. For almost a year after the incident, nothing we did was ever right. I needed to keep my eye on what was best for the students and make sure every "i" was dotted and every "t" was crossed. It can be very lonely at the top, especially when you have to make changes that cause people to lean into discomfort. Staff began to become quiet when I entered the room, and smoky backroom conferences were happening that were supportive of insubordination. Students were picking up on the mounting pressure in the building and noticed gaps in consistency. Change can be difficult, and leadership within that change can be taxing.

We slowly began to make notable progress that was acknowledged by the central office, and then my principal retired three months before the school year ended. At this point, I wanted the finish the school year and run 50,000,000 miles south to get away from being a school leader. I was offered the chance to become the school's principal, but I did not want it, because at that time, I felt like we were in a place where we needed change, and I wanted something different. I tried to go back into school social work. I filled out 164 applications, created separate resumes, and was willing to take the pay loss for a peace of mind. Needless to say, time was upon me. I had one child in college and another one going, the school needed a new principal, and he/she would be bringing new leadership staff. This transition meant out with the old in with the new.

My 165th application was submitted for a small contract high school that was looking for a new principal. The description of the school and how it was structured made me feel like this would be a win-win.

I immediately got an interview, and after a thorough process, I was offered the job. This transition offered the same question: who did I have to become to do what I needed to do for this position? I would now be the leader—the one responsible for everything—and I really had no time to waste. Everything I learned needed to be implemented and then some with a tone that put me in a position to lead from the front as suggested by authors Angie Morgan and Courtney Lynch. Their straightforward approach was what I needed to whip me into shape and become the example of what I was expecting from my staff. I needed to take accountability before I began to place blame and being a servant leader. School would be starting soon, and all eyes were on me.

Questions

1. Who have you had to become to do what you have done?

2. Is your becoming able to be sustained throughout your leadership role?

3. What did you learn about yourself that you didn't know before?

Lesson 4

Reintroductions

I have had to re-introduce myself to myself many times over the years. This was critical to make sure I wasn't holding people responsible for handling me a certain way and that I wasn't familiar with my own growth and development. I married young, each child changed my life, and my daily experiences have shaped who I am today. I have also made it a practice to reintroduce myself to my husband, children, mother, father, and other family members and friends. We leave our homes and travel to work and school, spend time with other people, and have a variety of experiences that we may not share. We may not even be aware of the impact they have had on our disposition and responses. Hence the importance of understanding how your day-to-day engagement directly impacts who you are and the constant need for reintroductions.

This experience with COVID-19 made everyone at some point or another take a hard stop. I took this time to reflect on where I am and if this is how I want to proceed with life after this stay at home is over. I have taken the time to reconnect with those closest to me and to be conscious of where everyone is in their life as well. During this time, it was also important for me to review what was driving me to be who I am and to determine whether it was still relevant at this time in my life. Interestingly enough, I found that a situation that occurred when I was in high school was a major impetus to my driven responses to things I am committed to in my life. I was a senior in high school, and my mother met with a very influential man to discuss what my financial possibilities could be for a four-year college or university. The gentleman reviewed my test scores, which were low, and gave his highly respected opinion. My mother came home, sat down, and informed me that the gentleman did not believe that she should waste her money on sending me to a four-year college or university. He also suggested that she send me to a junior college and then determine if I'm ready to go to a four-year college or university after I receive my Associate's degree.

I was offended by his statement to my mother, and I was also wondering if she even had an inkling of a thought that he just might be right. He had never met me, but I vowed to prove him wrong and destroy any concern in my mother's head about my ability to succeed in school based upon my test scores in high school. I applied to eight different universities—three in state and five out of state. I was accepted to seven out of the eight universities, but my mother was not able to afford for me to go out of state. I landed at Western Illinois University in Macomb, Illinois. I was placed on probation, and by the second semester, I was off probation and actively involved in five different activities on campus. I graduated in 1994 and sought the gentleman out to address his concerns and show him that you can't judge a book by its cover. In my reflection, I now see him as a vessel and not an individual trying to stop my greatness.

However, before that reflection began, his message resonated in my head for 30 years and drove me to secure degrees, certifications, and licenses that ultimately prepared me for God's work. I unconsciously kept trying to prove him wrong. I never wanted to feel that feeling again, but it was also time to let it go, to stop trying to prove what I can do, and to create a new authentic foundation. I gave myself permission to relax and celebrate my accomplishments. I also put myself on punishment. I am not allowed to secure one more degree, certificate, or license under the "just one more thing, then I'll be ready" justification. Ready for what? Ready for whom? Why is what I have not enough?

This effort has to be intentional, because if I am not consciously moving, my past will walk my walk for me.

This visceral work has driven me to really go through every layer of my life. I began asking all kinds of questions. Why did I marry who I married? Why did I choose my religion? Why did I pledge the sorority I'm in? How did I choose my major? Was I really happy? Was I on auto pilot? Whose life am I living? I thought about these questions because I have met so many people who have never really dug that deep. Would they do it all over the same way? If not, what would they do differently? If this isn't really me, then who am I?

Digging this deep helped me meet parts of myself that had not been touched in years. The reintroduction to my husband and adult children has been the most rewarding. I want to know the people around me, not their representative, and vice versa. I want my children to live a life that makes them happy, not one that I shape to make me feel good. Realizing that they are God's children whom He let borrow only gives me so much leverage in the first place. My mother-in-law and I were talking one day, and she said something to me that I will never forget: "I cannot wait for the day that [my son] wants to know me as a woman and not solely as his mother, as those two are or can be two separate things."

This life doesn't come with an instruction booklet, so many of us make mistakes with pure intentions. My own stuff got in my way, and no my life didn't turn out bad, but I know I missed a lot and sacrificed many moments that I will never get back. Reintroducing myself to myself and the people I love has helped me to refurbish, rehab and reset for the future. It is something I want to make sure I always do, as we are forever changing beings.

Questions

1. When was the last time you drilled down deep about what's driving you?

2. Is your original mission outdated?

3. Have your reintroduced yourself to the people who have been directly impacted by your journey?

Lesson 5

Sacrifice

The dictionary defines sacrifice as the act of giving up something valued for the sake of something else regarded as more important or worthy. As a servant leader, you have to sacrifice a lot of different things in a variety of areas to have successful outcomes. No matter what sacrifices you pick, eventually you have to provide an answer explaining why one thing was more important than the next. I have sacrificed myself, my mind, my body, and my soul. I have sacrificed time with my family, special moments where I was not present primarily because I was trying to get something done for something or someone else. I didn't believe that I had time to carve away if I was going to achieve the results I required as a leader.

Time with my parents and other family members and friends was also very limited. It is funny, because I currently teach a course to young adults helping them to understand the importance of time. I use money as an analogy, stating that you know your time is money, and once you lose it you can't get it back. We all get 86,400 seconds a day, and at that time, you get an opportunity to pick and choose what is really going to move you towards your goal. Once you are in the zone, it can be a serious rat race. The crazier part is that we can tell ourselves it is for our family, and somehow you really sacrifice the specific things that you said is valuable to you. I also teach a course that highlights the things you value. Most people find that their actions are not in alignment with the things they value. The actions are contradictory to the action of valuing something of importance.

As a leader, I have sacrificed many times, and initially, the outcome seemed grandiose. But when you get there and you are still not happy or you come out with the short end of the stick, you wonder if it was worth it. Motivational speaker and author Lisa Nichols speaks of this challenge in her book, *Abundance Now*. She wrote a piece about King Pyrrhus's victory over the Roman Army and what he sacrificed to win the war. She shared that that experience was called a Pyrrhic Victory, which is described as a person's ability to have amazing outcomes but losing the people they love in the midst. Everything about the Pyrrhic Victory deeply resonated with me and caused me to take responsibility for my choices. I have paid dearly for my choices, which is why I am able to write Green Panties, Ulcers, & Corns. I used everything

I had to do my job every day, and the unfair part is that by the time I got home, I had little to nothing left for the people I love.

My relationship with my husband suffered. I was completely depleted, so I am more than aware that there was a period of time when we were just going through the motions. President Barack Obama talked about wife calling him about ants in their house when he was trying to help run the country. Did she not know who he was? Couldn't she take care of the ants? Well, in reality, your family may know who you are, but they still have expectations of the relationship that you established prior to your blast-off. You must find a balance. I know it is hard, but it is worth it. At times, it may seem impossible, but this balance is worth it. You will have to delegate, shift around appointments, and sometimes just say "no."

In June 2018, I resigned from my position as a principal and went back to my first love providing support for the most at risk in my community. I have been on my new job for two years. I still am in a servant leadership position, but I am learning how to do it differently. Currently, I am in a different place with my children and my husband. Prior to COVID-19, my husband and I had an empty nest, and we reconnected with ourselves and with each other. But now our family is back together under the stay-at-home directive, which has forced us to give our relationship the undivided attention it needs before our adult children go their separate ways. My intention is to help servant leaders see what is ahead before they crash. Their sacrifice does not have to come with a destruction.

Questions

1. Have your sacrifices cost you the life you are working for?

2. What can you do to balance servant leadership and the attention your loved ones deserve?

3. Do you see yourself experiencing the Pyrrhic Victory? If so, how can you avoid losing yourself and those you love?

Lesson 6

Trajectory Changer

There is something really magical about being a trajectory changer. I am here to tell you that everyone, from infants to the elderly, has the power to change someone else's trajectory. People cannot fathom the impact of energy on every component of their life. From the time you wake up until the time you wake up again the next day, your energy will dictate how your day will go. Your energy will impact anyone you come across, including a stranger in the store, your partner, your spouse, your child, your client, a student, and/or a friend. The fact that you are a servant leader puts you in a position to be conscious of the fact that if you are not centered in the right place, that it could really impact someone and change their lives forever. For example, a leader in the class, whom we call the teacher, can make a statement to a student that negatively or positively changes their lives forever. According to the age of the individual, level of maturation, and self-esteem or confidence, your words, context, body language, or actions could ruin a person's life.

In a previous chapter, we talked about the gentleman who explained to my mother that he didn't believe that I was college material. That statement in itself changed the trajectory of my life, impacting me for 30 years. On a professional level, a leader can make or break a subordinate or co-worker. Your position of authority can automatically create an environment where the title implies that your words and actions have weight. You must monitor your auto pilot behavior and check your own emotions that may have been impacted by another trajectory changer that came across our path. Your perspective and perception have unspoken powers that can determine the outcome of your effectiveness.

As a trajectory changer, a bonus intention is to be a cultivator. When one is responsible for developing the minds of a team, a group, or future leaders, there is a never-ending search for the right way. The ultimate questions are: What is experience? Have you checked your perspective? You must develop an action plan based on differentiation. Our professional places are second homes to millions of people, and it is your responsibility to create a space that allows your team to be raw and authentic enough that we can see the core of their human potential, meet them where they are, and help them to develop the needed skills that will support their life purpose while fulfilling your mission and vision.

Rote traditional practices have their place in an environment but only to establish systematic foundations that connect human conversations before individuality takes over. We must take the time to understand whom we are leading, which means that we ultimately become the student. This, my friend, is where the rubber meets the road. Our workers, students, and customers come through the doors every morning carrying a variety of dynamics, emotions, experiences, and variations of beings. We made a conscious decision to play a major role in being responsible for their growth and development. This is not to be taken lightly and requires constant personal and professional development in order to show up and show out every day to bring the best out of the people we serve. They might not know who they are and the never-ending possibilities that are available to them if they move with purpose, have a plan, maneuver systems, build bridges, communicate effectively, and collaborate with others. Providing the proper training is an enlightening and reciprocal process, however it is almost seamless when we are willing to build relationships, increase our flexibility, and see our assignment as worthy. As a cultivator, provide access the best this world has to offer in their arena. Respect them, see them, and hear them for who they are and what they want to be.

Our work is cut out for us. We must remain steadfast in our efforts to cultivate our assignments. Our definition of progress must match their human potential. Our presence must give them strength and hope. Our attention will give them permission to soar with the understanding that our lack of attention creates mental and spiritual death. You are a trajectory changer; remember your power. You can change the world.

Questions

1. Do you see yourself as a trajectory changer?

2. Are you mindful of your energy and how it impacts others?

3. Do you realize that you see from your own perspective, which can determine how you respond to others?

Lesson 7

❋ ❋

Mind Your Own Business

While cleaning my room, I came across several personal action journals that I started, but unfortunately, I have not implemented most of the ideas. How many more eye-catching journals was I going to begin with little to no action behind my new epiphanies? Ironically, they all contained the same dreams and goals that have never been accomplished. I had lost respect for myself, even though I never failed to disappoint others as I proudly completed my commitments in helping them to fulfill their dreams. They were fully aware of what I was capable of, and I sold myself for the perfect price—all for them and none for me. I continued placing my dreams on the back burner, creating resentment for my unwavering dedication to someone else's success. This was twenty years of parking my car and being a passenger while consciously knowing that I should have been in the driver's seat.

I took all the right steps, surrounded myself with the right people, networked and followed through as

I invested in myself to do one more thing, and then I would say, "I think I'll be ready." I've invested a lot of money trying to get ready for my ultimate debut. Don't get me wrong, I took a few steps, had a couple of events, and received several accolades and applause, but something in me prevented me from going all the way and putting it all on the line. With several degrees, certificates, and licenses and over 25 years of experience in a variety of areas, what more did I need?

I needed to "mind my own business" with clarity, commitment, completion, and then celebration. I could do this and still be an authentic and responsible servant leader. My sanity and spiritual survival depended on me minding my own business. I had to embrace who I really was at my core, how I thought, what was the base of those thoughts, and why I was walking on the edge, scared to fall all the way in to my fullest expression. No one outside of myself could understand my eccentric thoughts and behavior, which initially caused me to always inquire for a second opinion. In my circles of influence, it seemed like my brain was going 50,000 miles per minute with phenomenal ideas with which I couldn't keep up and that I didn't know how to bring into reality. Eventually, I just let them pass like a scroll at the bottom of the television news screen, picking up one idea or another, settling for the easiest one. Settling for the one that wouldn't cause concern or discomfort to me or those in my immediate space. This road of least resistance was like a nightmare, playing over and over again with no ending because I didn't acknowledge its existence.

Every fiber of my being must be engaged to live out my fullest life, and the time has come to stop playing small. I made a decision to take 60 days, withdrawing from almost everything to reintroduce me to myself and I. I maintain an unlimited list of things I want to experience or do in life. One of these things is yoga. I initially wanted to take yoga to stay fit and increase my flexibility. I had inquired several times over a few years about teacher training, but never thought it would happen. While taking my introduction classes, I fell in love with the art of yoga and the residual, long-lasting effects after every class. I made a decision to sign up for teacher training, but what I got was a life-changing experience that I can't keep to myself.

This book is also about understanding that we are not here for ourselves—that we are chosen vessels that will deliver from the gifts and talents we have been given. Minding your own business gives you access to the fullest expression of your life. Minding your own business also comes with a cost that you cannot be afraid to embrace. I happened to find me within the four corners of my mat alongside an experience that changed the world.

When you mind your own business, you also engage in visceral authenticity. You really want to know who you are and how you came to be. You begin to prepare for a raw and rewarding journey. You must be ready to silence the outer noise to become familiar with your unique voice, likes and dislikes, wants and needs, and forgotten and buried thoughts. Circumstances, fears, and distractions have created shifts in our thinking that create layers of protection for our core. We consciously and unconsciously fight for our safety on every level, sometimes getting lost in the battle and reluctantly taking on characteristics that become a part of our daily facade. To feel pure authenticity is to be vulnerable and open to all that comes your way, knowing that you have the power to determine what something is, how you will respond, and where that response will take you.

This visceral process is more than a notion. Taking the time to drill down and gut out every area of your life places you in the driver's seat with full control. Everyone around you will not be supportive of your personal transformation and the undivided attention you give yourself while seeking out balance, fulfillment and happiness. Catching yourself when you begin to judge others, stopping the comparison game that weakens your core, deafening your ear to unsolicited criticism from yourself and others, and embracing constructive feedback results in you minding your own business and shuts out the distractions, which in turn increases your focus.

Building a strong foundation with no shortcuts increases your faith in yourself and your belief in what is ultimately possible. Your authentic self is powerful, phenomenal, and limitless, as it relates to helping you reach every goal and succeed in every domain of life. When you respect yourself, you become conscious of your time, relationships, choices, and where you plant your feet. You refuse to feel uncomfortable for the sake of others but remain flexible if your gifts and talents are required.

Visceral authenticity also requires that you acknowledge the role you have played in where you currently are in your life. Unconditionally loving yourself through the transparency but taking a firm stance against hoarding unhealthy actions or habits gives you room for improvements and transformation. Just about everyone at some point must take responsibility for minding their own business and ultimately enjoy the power to steer ourselves on the right path.

Questions

1. Have you been minding your own business?

2. In your service, have you forgotten your own goals and dreams?

3. Have you taken responsibility for where you are in your life?

Lesson 8

Who Helps the Helper?

Thousands of people have made a decision to be leaders, to give back, to educate, to train, to increase access, and to love on thousands of people around the world. As servant leaders, they shape our future, and it is rewarding to see them become leaders and contributing citizens in our society. As a servant leader, I am concerned about your mental and physical health when helping others is your mission and priority. People come to our spaces every day with a variety of emotions, including but not limited to happiness, conflict, excitement, detachment, eagerness, depression, love, hunger, and anger, but with our best efforts, we strive to keep them focused, growing, and dependable.

For servant leaders, it is never easy to meet everyone where they are; we come in early, leave late, take work home, and sacrifice the people we love for the job we perform. We must remember that self-preservation is the first law of nature. Many of us rent space in a fight-or-flight home during the unpredictable days. This can overwhelm your nervous system, causing a variety of issues. You must take care of yourself mentally, physically, and spiritually. In order to be your most productive, you can do the following:

1. Take the time early in the morning before everyone in our household rises for the day to sit in silence and first be thankful for what we have and then write out or think through our priorities for the day.

2. Get in 15-30 minutes of exercise.

3. Stay hydrated.

4. Eat or drink something nutritious to fuel your day.

5. During the day, shut your door, sit down, inhale and exhale deeply three to five times, complete a couple of basic stretches, and/or step outside for some fresh air.

6. Bring snacks to work that will give you energy and keep you balanced.

7. Go home and take a moment to love on your family.

8. Find a sacred place that you have created in your home to sit for a few minutes, breathe, and change into something more comfortable.

9. Before you go to sleep, think positive thoughts.

10. Do some nighttime yoga or stretches.

11. Sip on some chamomile tea.

12. Play a comforting tune.

13. Get at least six to eight hours of sleep per night.

Finding ways to balance your life, relax, and decrease stress are important for your survival. When you can relax you decrease your heart rate, your blood pressure normalizes and the body can function and repair itself. This allows you to regain energy, focus, and be motivated to do it all over again.

The helper is rarely asked what they need or checked on by those they serve. You must create a circle of accountability that forces you to live your best life in the midst of chaos. Your family and friends desire to have you after work, on the weekends, and after retirement. Yes, we must take 100 percent responsibility for our choice, but never for the price of declining health and mental suffering. Steal your moments to reflect on the white harvest of what you pour into the children whom you are charged to educate every day. You will be a better person, administrator, and educator if you can give on full instead of empty.

Striving to live authentically, consciously, and balanced is critical to achieving a positive result called well-being. The word "striving" should be duly noted as a verb, an action word that means one must fight for, struggle vigorously, or make great effort. Your life is worth fighting for to sustain a consistent or high level of happiness, peace, and good health. Staying aligned to or discovering your authentic self is one of the greatest accomplishments one can achieve. To know who you are, be clear about your why and exist with purpose. This creates an opportunity for you to be intentional about your aura, which ultimately determines your well-being.

Please understand that you are definitely a walking dictionary giving definition and meaning to every person, place, or thing that enters your space. The world is full of noise, and throughout our journey, we experience a variety of involuntary situations, good and bad, that keep us distracted from our internal and spiritual stability. We must take 100 percent responsibility for our responses to these invasions that, if left unchecked, can shift us from happy to unhappy, comfortable to uncomfortable, and good health to gravely ill without notice.

Auto-pilot living gives us permission to blame others and fall victim to haphazard outcomes. Turning off the cruise control, checking our own pulse, and sitting still requiring nothing else but oxygen will definitely help us to center ourselves and reset. Take time every day to take deep breaths, find a quiet place to settle your mind, engage in exercises that decrease your stress, take a walk, express gratitude, eat balanced meals, laugh, and love. Showing up in your full self increases your self-worth and your ability to live your life purpose touching those around you. There is no silver bullet for well-being, but the best part is you get to decide how much of your well-being you want to embrace.

Questions

1. Do you have someone on whom you can lean?

2. Are you in a position to delegate your work to balance your life?

3. Can you tell when you are overwhelmed or has your journey moved the needle?

Lesson 9

Simple Clarity Is Critical

Just about every major leader has pushed the world to know their "what" and their "why." Having clarity around what you want and why you are doing what you are doing gives you fuel to take and conquer every step to complete your goals. Your "what" may be to motivate others, help the homeless, or lose ten pounds. Your "why" may be your health, your family, your education, or any number of reasons, but these are the nucleus of the big picture—the driving force behind your sacrifice of time, presence and unwavering attention. Your what and why gets you out of bed, drives you to work, takes you to the gym, pushes you to ask a question or give an answer, drags you from bad habits, and helps you to make a decision.

Clarity supports your authenticity and helps you to get laser focused about your life. When things are crystal clear, all we need is courage to make a decision and move forward for implementation. It is a difficult and gruel-ing internal conflict when one mulls over situations or circumstances that are very clear. Fear can skew clarity.

Fear of being who you are and what that means to those around you can cause confusion, which slowly tears at the fabric of your being. A great example of this is if you were in a relationship and one of you sacrifices who you are to be in the space with the other. This ultimately ends in conflict because the relationship was not built on authenticity, which requires clarity and honesty.

When you are not clear and honest with yourself, you will waste a lot of time, resources, and energy. Being clear about your intentions and motivations increases your ability to take on the responsibility of your outcomes. No one else can be responsible for your decisions, which mirror your character traits and highlight your level of integrity. This is a lifetime journey of mindfulness that determines the outcome we desire. Clarity supports authenticity that comes with the responsibility of building character.

Questions

1. Are you clear about what you want from yourself, your life, your spouse, your children, and others?

2. Do you know why you want the what?

3. Is everyone around you clear about your what and why?

4. Do your actions match your answers?

About the Author

Necole K. Muhammad is a licensed clinical social worker, certified life coach, certified yoga teacher, certified sexologist, speaker, and professional development trainer. She is also a former high school administrator and a coauthor of the bestselling *Soul Talk, Vol. 3*. A doctoral candidate, Necole has her Master of Educational Leadership, Master of Social Work, and Bachelor of Science in Law Enforcement Administration.

Necole's mission is to help others live on their highest level. She is passionate about community service, and she is actively involved with Delta Sigma Theta Sorority, Incorporated; Top Ladies of Distinction; and the Sickle Cell Disease Association of Illinois. In her free time, Necole enjoys reading, yoga, dancing, and traveling. She is married with two adult children, a dog, and a cat. She lives in Chicago.

Learn more at www.necolemuhammad.com

purposely created
PUBLISHING

CREATING DISTINCTIVE BOOKS
WITH INTENTIONAL RESULTS

We're a collaborative group of creative masterminds
with a mission to produce high-quality books to position
you for monumental success in the marketplace.

Our professional team of writers, editors, designers,
and marketing strategists work closely together to ensure
that every detail of your book is a clear representation
of the message in your writing.

Want to know more?
Write to us at info@publishyourgift.com
or call (888) 949-6228

Discover great books, exclusive offers, and more at
www.PublishYourGift.com

Connect with us on social media

@publishyourgift

CPSIA information can be obtained
at www.ICGtesting.com
Printed in the USA
LVHW010229150121
676361LV00013B/677

9 781644 842898